chihuahu

understanding and
caring for your breed

C000294975

Written by
Christine Davies

chihuahua

understanding and
caring for your breed

Written by
Christine Davies

Pet Book Publishing Company

Bishton Farm, Bishton Lane, Chepstow, NP16 7LG, United Kingdom.
881 Harmony Road, Unit A, Eatonton, GA31024 United States of America.

Printed and bound in China through Printworks International.

ISBN: 978-1-906305-76-5
ISBN: 1-906305-76-5

Acknowledgements

The publishers would like to thank the following for help with
photography: David Milton (Gestavo), Pat Milton (Cleopy), Margaret
Greening (Hamaja), and Pat Cullen (Culcia).

Contents

Introducing the Chihuahua

Small is beautiful, and that is certainly true of the tiny Chihuahua, the smallest dog breed in the world. But this captivating little creature is no pushover. The Chihuahua exudes self-importance, and demands to be taken seriously.

The Chihuahua is one of the most ancient of breeds and during his long history he has become the most perfect companion dog. Once you have owned a Chi, no other breed will do.

Physical characterstics

Despite his small size, the Chihuahua is a sturdy, well-proportioned dog, slightly longer in the body than his height at the shoulders. He moves with

purpose, his head held high and his tail slightly curved over his body, with an air that says: "look at me!"

The Chihuahua is known as a head breed, meaning that this is an outstanding feature, making the Chi unique in the dog world. The skull is apple-domed, and this is set off by large, flaring ears. The Chi's dark eyes shine with love and devotion, or with mischief!

If you like grooming, you can choose the long-coated Chi, otherwise the smooth-coat will be your dog of choice. Both varieties come in a wonderful array of colors.

The molera

The Chihuahua has a molera, or open fontanelle, which is a unique breed characteristic. In other breeds – and in human babies – the frontal and parietal bones of the cranium fuse soon after birth. In the case of the Chihuahua, the bones may not fuse until later, and in some cases it remains an open fontanelle. It is reckoned that the bones will fuse in 50 per cent of Chihuahua by the time they are three years old.

An open fontanelle should not be considered a defect, but dogs should be treated with extra care as the head is more vulnerable.

Temperament

The Chihuahua has no doubt in his mind: he is a proper dog, and he wants to be treated as such. He may be small, but he is ready to take on the world. He is active, inquisitive and intelligent, and he relishes the opportunity to use his brain.

Of course, he likes his cuddles, and will be a devoted companion, but he does not want to be treated like a pampered baby who never has the chance to enjoy doggy pursuits.

Unfortunately the tiny Chi has become the victim of a fashion fad for 'handbag dogs', and celebrities such as Paris Hilton, Madonna and Britney Spears have all been photographed carrying their Chihuahuas as fashion accessories. This is no life for a dog; the Chihuahua should be valued for what he is – a superb companion, but a dog at heart.

The ideal home

Town or country, mansion or apartment, the Chihuahua will be happy as long as he has company. This is a breed that thrives on being part of a family and joining in all activities. He is an ideal choice for older owners as his exercise requirements are minimal, but he will also enjoy life with a younger family. As he is small, and therefore more vulnerable to injury, he is not a good choice for families with very small children.

The Chihuahua is totally fearless, and will mix with other, larger breeds. Indeed, he usually ends up the boss! However, care should be taken with initial interactions.

Beware, Chihuahuas are very collectible, and although you may start off with one, you may soon find yourself with a mini tribe of Chis!

Life expectancy

Toy dogs tend to have a good life expectancy, and the Chihuahua does better than most. With luck, a Chi will survive into his teens. A good few make it to their mid teens, and there are even a few that reach their late teens and still enjoy a good quality of life.

Tracing back in time

The Chihuahua has a long and tangled history, and it is sometimes hard to separate fact from fiction. There are colorful tales, now shrouded in the mists of time, making the Chihuahua the most fascinating of breeds.

There are two schools of thought as to where the Chihuahua came from. Both are equally plausible, so you can take your pick!

Mexican roots

The Chihuahua gets its name from the northern part of Mexico, bordering on Texas, Arizona and New Mexico, which bears the same name. The earliest archaeological evidence dates back to the 5th Century AD. The Mayan Indians made clay sculptures of small dogs which do look like the Chihuahuas we know today.

In AD1100 Central American Indians, known as Toltecs, conquered the southern and central parts of Mexico. They kept pet dogs, some long-haired, which they called Techichi. They were highly valued as house dogs, and were also used in religious ceremonies.

In 1325 the Aztecs conquered the Toltecs and established their own civilisation which was to last until 1521. The descendants of the Techichi played an important part in their culture. When a person died, a yellow or red dog was sacrificed so he could accompany the dead person on his journey to the afterlife. This explains why many graves excavated in Mexico contained the skeletons of small dogs.

There is a gap in the Techichi's story following the Spanish conquest. Some believe they went feral and survived by hunting small rodents. Others think it is more likely that they were crossed with the black and tan terrier type dogs that the Spanish brought with them. But is was to be over 300 years before the little dog from Mexico was next heard of.

The Mediterranean theory

The origins of many of our Toy dogs can be traced
to the Mediterranean, and there is a theory that the
ancestors of the Chihuahua were found on the island
of Malta. It is known that dogs with the molera trait
(the soft spot on the skull unique to the Chihuahua),
came from Malta and were taken on trading ships to
other parts of Europe. Evidence of this comes from
European paintings of the period; there is
even a tiny dog, resembling a Chihuahua,
featured on a fresco in the Sistine Chapel in
Rome.

*The Xoloitzcuintle: One
of the ancient breeds
of Mexico.*

Developing the breed

We now take a great leap forward to the 1850s when small dogs were found living in Mexico. Some were smooth-coated, some long-coated, and some hairless (later to become the Mexican hairless).

Some of these dogs were taken to the United States, where they were known as Arizona dogs or Texas dogs. Later the smooth and long-coated varieties were christened the Mexican Chihuahua, after the Mexican state where they were discovered.

Show debut

In 1884 the first Chihuahua was exhibited in the American show ring; it was entered in the Miscellaneous Class as a Chihuahua Terrier.

James Watson, a well-known American judge and author of *The Dog Book*, gives an account of the Chihuahua in 1888, describing it as a small,

smooth-coated terrier, with a molera and a flat tail. It is interesting to note that all the early show dogs were smooth-coated, and many regard them as the original Chihuahua.

At this stage the breed appears to have come in different sizes, and in a variety of colours, all based on imports from Mexico. Its popularity grew, but the turning point came with the establishment of the Chihuahua Club of America in 1923, and, with it, the adoption of the first official Breed Standard.

There are records of Chihuahuas being kept as pets in the UK as early as 1850, but it was not until 1895 that a Chihuahua was exhibited at a show. This was a little dog called Theo, and he made his debut at the Ladies Kennel Association – the first show organised by women.

Two varieties

Long-coated and smooth-coated Chihuahuas were shown together in the USA until 1952; at that point the long-coat was made a separate variety, and the first club specifically for long-coats was established.

In the UK, the two varieties were not separated until 1965. The long-coated variety was based on imports from the US, but some Toy breeds were infused in an attempt to improve coats. Interbreeding between

Papillons and Pomeranians took place up until the 1940s, and subtle signs of these two breeds can still crop up in some bloodlines.

The breed today

The smooth-coated Chihuahua remains the most popular of the two varieties, but the long-coat also has a devoted following. The Chihuahua is currently ranked as the 14th most popular breed in the US, and it is ranked in the top 10 in many other countries worldwide.

The Papillon was one of the breeds used in the development of the long-coated Chihuahua.

What should a Chihuahua look like?

Small and dainty, the Chihuahua is a real crowd pleaser as he struts out with the confidence of a dog ten times his size.

So what makes the Chihuahua so special?

The Chihuahua has an ancient lineage, but the breed as we know it today has been with us for just over a century. Since official recognition, breeders have been striving to produce dogs that retain the appearance and characteristics so highly valued in the show ring and by pet owners. To achieve this, they are guided by a Breed Standard, which is a written blueprint describing what the perfect specimen should look like.

Of course, there is no such thing as a 'perfect' dog,

but breeders aspire to produce dogs that conform as closely as possible to the picture in words presented in the Breed Standard. In the show ring, judges use the Breed Standard to assess the dogs that come before them, and it is the dog that, in their opinion, comes closest to the ideal, that will win top honours.

This has significance beyond the sport of showing for it is the dogs that win in the ring that will be used for breeding. The winners of today are therefore responsible for passing on their genes to future generations and preserving the breed in its best form.

There are some differences in the wording of the Breed Standard depending on national kennel clubs. The American Kennel Club and the Federation Cynologique Internationale, which is the governing body for 86 countries, have far more descriptive Standards than the brief outline given in the English version. However the UK Breed Standard is prefaced with a statement that all dogs must be "fit for function". This means that dogs of all breeds should have the conformation that would enable them to fulfil their original working role.

You may think that this does not apply to the Chihuahua, as the breed was developed to be a companion dog. But the underlying purpose of "fit for function" is that dogs are bred without

Points of anatomy

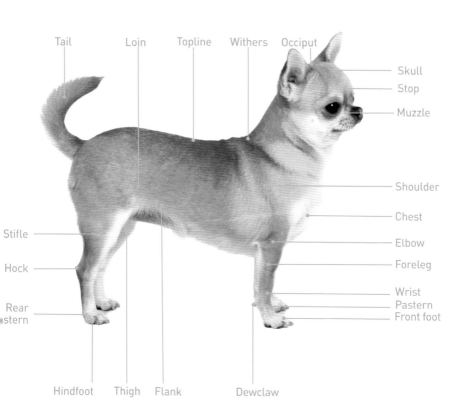

Tail · Loin · Topline · Withers · Occiput · Skull · Stop · Muzzle · Shoulder · Chest · Elbow · Foreleg · Wrist · Pastern · Front foot · Stifle · Hock · Rear pastern · Hindfoot · Thigh · Flank · Dewclaw

exaggerations, which could be detrimental to their health, welfare or soundness.

General appearance

The Chihuahua is a little dog, with a compact body. The length of the body is slightly longer than the height at the shoulders, making him slightly "off square". He is alert, with a saucy expression, and although he moves with grace, his action is swift and forceful.

Temperament

It is hard to sum up the unique Chihuahua temperament in just a few words but the key words are 'gay', 'spirited' and 'intelligent'. The American Standard makes a comparison with terriers, stating that the Chihuahua shares the same qualities of confidence, self-importance and self-reliance.

Head

The head is a defining feature of the breed; a Chihuahua would not be a Chihuahua without the typical 'apple dome' skull. The muzzle is short and slightly pointed, and the stop – the step-up between the muzzle and the forehead – is well defined. The cheeks appear clean and the lips are lean and close fitting.

Facing page: The apple-domed skull and flaring ears are important breed features.

Eyes

In a small face, the eyes are an important feature, and this is particularly true of the Chihuahua. His eyes are large and round; they should be set well apart and should not protrude from the skull. Although light eyes in light colored dogs are allowed, dark or ruby eyes tend to be more expressive and help to give the Chi his "saucy" look.

Ears

The large, flaring ears, set on the apple-domed skull, look truly spectacular. They are positioned at an angle of approximately 45 degrees, giving good breadth between them. They are carried erect; broad at the base, tapering gradually towards a slightly rounded tip. Tipped ears are considered a serious fault.

Mouth

The jaws are strong and the teeth should meet in a scissor bite, meaning the teeth on the upper jaw should closely overlap the teeth on the lower jaw. The American and FCI Standards also allow a level or 'pincer' bite where the upper and lower incisor teeth meet each other edge to edge.

Neck

The neck is slightly arched, sloping into clean cut shoulders. It is of medium length, slightly thicker in males than in females.

Forequarters

The shoulders slope into slightly broadening support of the straight front legs. The front legs are set well under the chest to give freedom of movement. The elbows are firm and fit close to the body, which also helps to produce the correct movement.

The two varieties – long-coated and smooth-coated – are identical in conformation. The only difference is in their coat.

Body

The topline is level and the ribs are rounded, but not so much that the dog appears barrel-shaped. The underline – more evident on smooths – should show a clear tuck-up. The body should be slightly longer than the height of the dog, but some leeway is given to bitches, because a longer back will make breeding easier as she will have more room.

Hindquarters

The hindquarters should be muscular, with good angulation. The hocks, the 'ankle' joints, should be set well apart, turning neither in nor out.

Feet

As befits his size, the Chihuahua has small, dainty feet. The toes should be well divided, but not spread out. The pads are cushioned; the pasterns, which act as shock absorbers on the front legs, are strong and flexible.

Tail

Seeing a Chihuahua trotting out, with his tail held high, is a pure delight. It sums up the breed's air of purpose and self-importance.

The tail may look different in a long-coated Chihuahua because of the abundant feathering but, in fact, it is identical to the smooth-coat's in terms of size, shape and carriage. It is medium in length, set high and carried over the back, described as a 'sickle' tail. It is fairly flat, broadening in the centre and tapering to a point.

Gait/movement

Despite his diminutive size, the Chihuahua should move with a brisk, forceful action. He should have good reach in front, with the drive coming from the hindquarters. His top-line should remain firm and level when he is moving.

Coat

The smooth-coated Chihuahua has a short, glossy coat that is soft in texture and lies close to the skin. An undercoat and a ruff is allowed; in the American Standard a ruff is "preferred".

In the long-coated variety, the coat is also soft in texture and may lie flat, or be slightly wavy. There is feathering on the ears, feet and legs, plus the "pants" on the hindquarters. There is a large ruff on the neck and the feathering on the tail is plume-like.

Color

The Chihuahua can be any color – solid or marked. In the UK, the Kennel Club will not register merle (dapple) puppies, nor the progeny from merle parents. The reason is because the color is associated with congenital faults such as deafness and blindness. Research has shown that the merle gene is not found in Chihuahuas, which points to the fact that merle Chihuahuas cannot be pure-bred.

Size

There has been considerable debate over the size of Chihuahuas, as there was a preference for tiny dogs, weighing between 1 and 4lb (0.5 to 1.8 kg). The UK Standard even stated: "If two dogs are equally good in type, the more diminutive is preferred".

This was having a major impact on health issues, particularly in relation to whelping, and now the requirement is for dogs up to 6lb (2.7kg), with 4 to 6lb (1.8 to 2.7 kg) being preferred. The American Standard keeps it simple, asking for "a well-balanced little dog not to exceed 6lb". The FCI has a wider range, accepting dogs between 1.5 and 3kg.

Summing up

Although the majority of Chihuahuas are pet dogs and will never be exhibited in the show ring, it is important that breeders strive for perfection and try to produce dogs that adhere as closely as possible to the Breed Standard. This ensures that the Chi remains sound in mind and body, and retains his unique characteristics.

Facing page: Size may have an impact on a Chihuahua's health and well-being.

What do you want from your Chihuahua?

There are hundreds of dog breeds to choose from, so how can you be sure that the Chihuahua is the right breed for you? Before you take the plunge into Chi ownership, weigh up the pros and cons so you can be 100 per cent confident that this is the breed best suited to your lifestyle.

Companion

Throughout his long history, the Chihuahua has been prized for his very special brand of companionship, and this remains true to this day. He is a people dog, and his *raison d'etre* is to be with his beloved family. He takes his role in the family very seriously, seeing himself as both watch dog and companion.

But bear in mind that companionship comes at a price, and a Chihuahua will be thoroughly miserable if he is left for lengthy periods or excluded from family activities. A Chihuahua is so small he can accompany you almost anywhere, which will give you both a lot of pleasure.

This is a breed that will suit a wide variety of owners, but if you have small children, it may be better to delay Chi ownership until they are a little older. Toddlers are naturally clumsy, and if they get over-excited, games can get out of hand very easily. A tiny puppy cannot withstand rough handling, no matter how unintentional it is.

If you are getting on in years, a Chihuahua will be a loving companion, alternating periods of activity with times when he is happy to chill out with you. But bear in mind that this is a small dog that can move at speed, so he may not be ideal for those who are frail.

Show dog

Do you have ambitions to exhibit your Chihuahua in the show ring? This is a specialist sport, which often becomes highly addictive, but you do need the right dog to start with.

If you plan to show your Chihuahua, you need to track down a show quality puppy, and train him so he will perform in the show ring, and accept the detailed 'hands on' examination that he will be subjected to when he is being judged.

The smooth-coat is easy to present in the show ring in terms of grooming; the workload steps up with a long-coated Chihuahua, but it is still relatively straightforward compared to some of the other long-coated Toy breeds.

It is also important to bear in mind that not every puppy with show potential develops into a top-quality specimen, and so you must be prepared to love your Chihuahua and give him a home for life, even if he doesn't make the grade.

Sports dog

This Chihuahua's size imposes obvious limitations, but there are possibilities if you want to get involved in specialized training. See Opportunities for Chihuahuas, page 150.

Facing page: The Chi is a clever dog and can be trained to a high level.

What does your Chihuahua want from you?

A dog cannot speak for himself, so we need to view the world from a canine perspective and work out what a Chihuahua needs in order to live a happy, contented and fulfilling life.

Time and commitment

First of all, a Chihuahua needs a commitment that you will care for him for the duration of his life – guiding him through his puppyhood, enjoying his adulthood, and being there for him in his later years. If all potential owners were prepared to make this pledge, there would be scarcely any dogs in rescue.

The Chihuahua was bred to be a companion dog, and this is what he must be. If you cannot give your

Chihuahua the time and commitment he deserves, you would be strongly advised to delay owning a dog until your circumstances change.

Remember, no dog of any breed should be left on his own for longer than four hours. If work, or other commitments, mean you have to leave your dog for longer, you will need to make suitable arrangements. Doggy day care is a viable option, but you would have to make sure that the facilities and staff were up to standard, and that your Chihuahua would be mixed with dogs of appropriate size and of sound temperament.

Practical matters

The Chihuahua is relatively easy to care for, but this is not always the best news for a breed. A dog of this size will fit into any home, he will not be expensive to feed, he requires minimal exercise, and it is only the long-coated variety that is demanding in terms of coat care.

However, if your criteria for a dog depend on how little you need to do, perhaps you should reconsider whether you really want a dog in your life. A dog – even one as small as a Chihuahua – needs input from you, and this should be considered a top priority.

Mental stimulation

The Chihuahua does not need much in the way of physical exercise, but this highly intelligent little dog does require mental stimulation to keep his brain occupied. Your Chihuahua must always be treated with dignity and respect; the fashion for keeping Chis as 'handbag dogs' should be utterly rejected.

As a Chihuahua owner, you must take responsibility for your dog's mental wellbeing.
It does not matter what you to with him – training exercises, teaching tricks, trips out in the car, or going for new, interesting walks – all are equally appreciated, and will give your Chi a purpose in life.

You also need to provide a sense of leadership so your Chihuahua knows you are the decision-maker in the family. A little basic training, and consistency in observing house rules, is all that is required. For more information, see page 130.

A Chi may be tiny, but he should be treated like a proper dog – and never as a fashion accessory.

Extra
considerations

Now you have decided that a Chihuahua is the dog of your dreams, you can narrow your choice so you know exactly what you are looking for.

Long-coat or smooth-coat?

This is entirely a matter of personal preference; the two varieties are identical in everything except coat. However, Chi owners tend to stick to their chosen variety. Some love the clean cut lines of the smooth, others find the softer appearance of the long-coat more appealing.

If you opt for a long-coat, you will need to dedicate time to regular grooming sessions as the feathering on this soft textured coat can tangle very easily.

Color

The Chihuahua can be any color, although the paler colors – whites, creams and fawns – plus black and tans are generally more successful in the show ring. Particolors (white plus a solid color) are popular in the US, but are rarely seen in the UK. Beware of blues and dapples as there are associated health risks with these colors. See Breed-Specific Conditions, page 182.

Male or female?

There is no difference in size between males and females, so it all comes down to temperament. In the Chihuahua world, the general belief is that males are a little more people orientated than females. They form a strong bond with their owners, some say, particularly with women, and are very loving. Females are often more independent, sometimes a little more spirited. But they also sweet natured and affectionate and will become an integral member of the family. When it comes down to it, all dogs are individuals, so you can never second-guess how a Chi will turn out.

If you opt for a female, you will have to cope with her seasonal cycle, which will start at eight months or nine months, although some may be as late as 14-15 months. Following her first season, she will come into season at six to nine monthly intervals thereafter. During the three-week period of a season, you will need to keep your bitch away from entire males (males that have not been neutered) to eliminate the risk of an unwanted pregnancy.

Many pet owners opt for neutering, which puts an end to the seasons, and also has many attendant health benefits. The operation, known as spaying, is usually carried out at some point after the first season. The best plan is to seek advice from your vet.

An entire male may not cause many problems, although some do have a stronger tendency to mark, which could include the house. However, training will usually put a stop to this. An entire male will also be on the lookout for bitches in season, and this may lead to difficulties, depending on your circumstances.

Neutering (castrating) a male is a relatively simple operation, and there are associated health benefits. Again, you should seek advice from your vet.

More than one?

Chihuahuas are sociable dogs and certainly enjoy each other's company. But you would be wise to guard against the temptation of getting two puppies of similar ages, or two from the same litter.

Unfortunately there are some unscrupulous breeders who encourage people to do this, but they are thinking purely in terms of profit, and not considering the welfare of the puppies.

Looking after one puppy is hard work, but taking on two pups at the same time is more than double the workload. House training is a nightmare as, often, you don't even know which puppy is making mistakes, and training is impossible unless you separate the two puppies and give them one-on-one attention.

The puppies will never be bored as they have each other to play with. However, the likelihood is that they will form a close bond, and you will come a poor second.

If you do decide to add to your Chihuahua population, wait at least 18 months so your first dog is fully trained and settled before taking on a puppy.

Getting two puppies of the same age is a recipe for disaster.

An older dog

You may decide to miss out on the puppy phase and take on an older dog instead. Such a dog may be harder to track down, but sometimes a breeder may have a youngster that is not suitable for showing, but is perfect for a family pet. In some cases, a breeder may rehome a female when her breeding career is at an end so she will enjoy the benefits of getting more individual attention.

There are advantages to taking on an older dog, as you know exactly what you are getting. But the upheaval of changing homes can be quite upsetting, so you will need to have plenty of patience during the settling in period.

Rehoming a rescued dog

We are fortunate that the number of Chihuahuas that end up in rescue is relatively small, and this is often through no fault of the dog. The reasons are various, ranging from illness or death of the original owner to family breakdown, changing jobs, or even the arrival of a new baby.

It is unlikely that you will find a purebred in an all breed rescue centre, but the specialist breed clubs run rescue schemes, and this will be your best option if you decide to go down this route.

Try to find out as much as you can about a dog's history so you know exactly what you are taking on. You need to be realistic about what you are capable of achieving so you can be sure you can give the dog in question a permanent home.

Again, you need to give a rescued Chihuahua plenty of time and patience as he settles into his new home, but if all goes well, you will have the reward of knowing that you have given your dog a second chance.

Can you give a rescued Chi a second chance?

Sourcing a puppy

Your aim is to find a healthy puppy that is typical of the breed, and has been reared with the greatest possible care. Where to start?

A tried-and-trusted method of finding a puppy is to attend a dog show where your chosen breed is being exhibited. This will give you the opportunity to see lots of different Chihuahuas, both long-coats and smooth-coats. Apart from the obvious differences in coat and color, you may think there is little to choose between the dogs you see in the ring. However, when you look closer, you notice there are different 'types' on show. They are all purebred Chihuahuas, but breeders produce dogs with a family likeness, and so you can see which type you prefer.

When judging has been completed, talk to the exhibitors and find out more about their dogs. They may not have puppies available, but some will be planning a litter, and you may decide to put your name on a waiting list.

Internet research

The Internet is an excellent resource, but when it comes to finding a puppy, use it with care:

DO go to the website of your national Kennel Club.

Both the American Kennel Club (AKC) and the Kennel Club (KC) have excellent websites that will give you information about the Chihuahua as a breed, and what to look for when choosing a puppy. You will also find contact details for specialist breed clubs (see below).

Both sites have lists of puppies available, and you can look out for breeders of merit (AKC) and assured breeders (KC) which indicates that a code of conduct has been adhered to.

DO find details of specialist breed clubs.

On breed club websites you will find lots of useful information that will help you to care for your Chihuahua. There may be contact details of breeders in your area, or you may need to go through the club secretary. Some websites also have a list of breeders who have puppies available. The advantage of going through a breed club is that members will follow a code of ethics, and this will give you some guarantees regarding breeding stock and health checks.

DO NOT look at puppies for sale.

There are legitimate Chihuahua breeders with their own websites, and they may, occasionally, advertise a litter, although in most cases reputable breeders have waiting lists for their puppies. The danger comes from unscrupulous breeders who produce puppies purely for profit, with no thought for the health of the dogs they breed from and no care given to rearing the litter. Photos of puppies are hard to resist, but never make a decision based purely on an advertisement. You need to find out who the breeder is, and have the opportunity to visit their premises and inspect the litter before making a decision.

Questions, questions, questions

When you find a breeder with puppies available, you will have lots of questions to ask. These should include the following:

- Where have the puppies been reared? Hopefully, they will be in a home environment, which gives them the best possible start in life.

- How many are in the litter?

- What colors are available?

- What is the split of males and females?

- How many have already been spoken for? The breeder will probably be keeping a puppy to show or for breeding, and there may be other prospective purchasers on a waiting list.

- Can I see the mother with her puppies?

- What age are the puppies?

- When will they be ready to go to their new homes?

Bear in mind that puppies need to be with their mother and siblings until they are at least eight weeks of age, otherwise they miss out on vital learning and communication skills which will have a detrimental effect on them for the rest of their lives. Most breeders of Toy dogs prefer to keep the puppies a little longer – until they are 10-12 weeks of age – when they are bigger and ready to face the world.

You should also be prepared to answer a number of searching questions so the breeder can check if you are suitable as a potential owner of one of their precious puppies.

You will be asked some or all of the following questions:

- What is your home set up?

- Do you have children/grandchildren?

- What are their ages?

- Is there somebody at home the majority of the time?

- Do you already own a dog?

- What breed is it?

- What is your previous experience with dogs?

- Do you have plans to show your Chihuahua?

Bear in mind, there is no such thing as a 'teacup' dog – an extra small Chi, sometimes offered at a higher price, will usually be the runt of the litter.

Be very wary of a breeder who does not ask you questions. He or she may be more interested in making money out of the puppies than ensuring that they go to good homes. The breeder may also have taken other short cuts which may prove disastrous, and very expensive, in terms of vet bills or plain heartache.

Health issues

In common with all purebred dogs, the Chihuahua suffers from a few hereditary problems. There are no health tests required for breeding stock at the moment, but you would be advised to talk to the breeder about the health status of their dogs and find out if there are any issues of concern. For information on inherited conditions, see page 182.

Puppy
watching

When you see a litter of Chihuahua puppies, you will be well and truly smitten! These beautiful little creatures are tiny versions of adult dogs, and they are simply bursting with personality. However, you must not let your heart rule your head; try to put your feelings to one side so you can make an informed choice. You need to be 100 per cent confident that the breeding stock is healthy, and the puppies have been reared with love and care, before making a commitment to buy.

Viewing a litter

It is a good idea to have a mental checklist of what to look out for when you visit a breeder. You want to see:

- A clean, hygienic environment.

- Puppies that are out-going and friendly, and eager to meet you.

- A sweet-natured mother ready to show off her pups.

- Puppies that are well covered, but not pot-bellied, which could be an indication of worms.

- Bright eyes, with no sign of soreness or discharge.

- Clean ears that smell fresh.

- No discharge from the nose.

- Clean rear ends – matting could indicate upset tummies.

- Lively pups that are keen to play.

It is important that you see the mother with her puppies as this will give you a good idea of the temperament they are likely to inherit. It is also helpful if you can meet other close relatives so you can see the type of Chihuahua the breeder produces.

In most cases, you will not be able to see the father (sire) as most breeders will travel some distance to find a stud dog that is not too close to their own bloodlines and complements their bitch. However, you should be able to see photos of him and be given the chance to examine his pedigree and show record.

Companion puppy

If you are looking for a Chihuahua as a companion, you should be guided by the breeder, who will have spent hours and hours puppy watching, and will know each of the pups as individuals. It is tempting to choose a puppy yourself, but the breeder will take into account your family set up and lifestyle and will help you to pick the most suitable puppy.

Show puppy

If you are buying a puppy with the hope of showing him, make sure you make this clear to the breeder. A lot of planning goes into producing a litter, and although all the puppies will have been reared with equal care, there will be one or two that have show potential.

Ideally, recruit a breed expert to inspect the puppies with you, so you have the benefit of their objective evaluation. The breeder will also be there to help as they will want to ensure that only the best of their stock is exhibited in the show ring.

It is best to wait until the puppies are at least eight weeks old before making an assessment of show potential.

Look out for a puppy with the following attributes:

- Apple-domed head. This should be evident from two weeks of age.

- Large, lustrous eyes.

- Large, flaring ears. They should be erect by eight weeks, although they may go through an unsettled stage when a puppy is teething.

- Teeth should meet in a scissor or level bite (see page 28), although this cannot be guaranteed to remain correct until the adult teeth come in.

- A sturdy body that is in proportion.

- Movement should be free and purposeful – a puppy that is put together correctly will move correctly.

- An extrovert, out-going temperament.

It is important to bear in mind that puppies go through many phases as they are developing. A promising puppy may well go through an ugly duckling phase, and all you can do is hope that he blossoms! However, if your Chihuahua fails to make the grade in the show ring, he will still be an outstanding companion who will be a much-loved member of your family.

A Chihuahua-friendly home

It may seem an age before your Chihuahua puppy is ready to leave the breeder and move to his new home. But you can fill the time by getting your home ready, and buying the equipment you will need.

These preparations apply to a new puppy but, in reality, they are the means of creating an environment that is safe and secure for your Chi throughout his life.

In the home

If you think that a tiny Chihuahua puppy will not make a big impact on your home, think again. A small puppy that moves at lightning speed can get himself into all sorts of trouble, so safety is the key issue.

The best plan is to decide which rooms your Chihuahua will have access to, and make these areas puppy friendly.

Trailing electric cables are a major hazard and these will need to be secured out of reach. You will need to make sure all cupboards are secure, particularly in the kitchen, where you may store cleaning materials that could be toxic to dogs. Household plants can also be poisonous, so these will need to relocated, along with breakable ornaments.

Your puppy will be too small to negotiate stairs to begin with, so it may be easier to make upstairs off-limits right from the start. The best way of doing this is to use a baby gate, making sure your puppy cannot squeeze through, which could result in injury.

In the garden

You may think that secure fencing is only a necessity for large dogs, but Chihuahuas are great escapologists and you will be amazed at how high they can jump. If they can't get over, they will try going under, and they will have no problem squeezing through the smallest of gaps. You will therefore need to check all boundary fencing, just in case your Chihuahua finds an escape route. Gates leading from the garden should have secure fastenings.

The Chihuahua is a great explorer so potential hazards, such as a garden pond or swimming pool, must be strictly off limits. There are a number of flowers and shrubs that are toxic to dogs, so check this out on the Internet or by seeking advice from your local garden centre. A list is available at www.dogbooksonline.co.uk/caring/poisonous-plants/

You will also need to designate a toileting area. This will assist the house-training process, and it will also make cleaning up easier. For information on house-training, see page 94.

House rules

Before your puppy comes home, hold a family conference to decide on the house rules. For example, is your Chihuahua going to be allowed to roam downstairs, or will you keep him in the kitchen unless you can supervise him elsewhere?

Doubtless your Chi will be allowed on your lap for a cuddle, but he will, therefore, presume that he is allowed on the sofa whenever he chooses. You may be happy with this, but if you want to establish no go areas, you should set the rules and keep to them from day one. Once you have allowed your puppy to do something once, he will think that this is 'allowed', regardless of whether you change your mind. You and your family must make decisions – and stick with them – otherwise your puppy will be upset and confused, not understanding what you want of him.

Buying equipment

There are some essential items of equipment you will need for your Chihuahua. If you choose wisely, much of it will last for many years.

Indoor crate

Rearing a puppy is so much easier if you invest in an indoor crate. It provides a safe haven for your puppy at night, when you have to go out during the day, and at other times when you cannot supervise him. A puppy needs a base where he feels safe and secure, and where he can rest undisturbed. An indoor crate provides the perfect den, and many adults continue to use them throughout their lives.

You will also need to consider where you are going to locate the crate. The kitchen is usually the most suitable place, as this is the hub of family life. Try to find a snug corner where the puppy can rest when he wants to, but where he can also see what is going on around him, and still be with the family.

The Chihuahua may be small, but that does not stop him getting up to all sorts of mischief...

Beds and bedding

The crate will need to be lined with bedding and the best type to buy is synthetic fleece. This is warm and cosy, and, as moisture soaks through it, your puppy will not have a wet bed when he is tiny and is still unable to go through the night without relieving himself. This type of bedding is machine washable and easy to dry. Buy two pieces, so you have one to use while the other is in the wash.

If you have purchased a crate, you may not feel the need to buy an extra bed, although many Chis like to have a bed in the family room so they feel part of household activities. There is an amazing array of dog-beds to chose from – duvets, bean bags, cushions, baskets, igloos, mini-four posters – so you can take your pick! Before you make a major investment, wait until your puppy has gone through the chewing phase; you will be surprised at how much damage can be inflicted by small teeth.

Playpen

A puppy playpen, sold at most pet retailers, provides a bigger base for your Chihuahua. There will be room for a bed and a play area, giving your Chi the freedom to move around while remaining safe and secure.

Collar and leash

You may think that it is not worth buying a collar for the first few weeks, but the sooner your pup gets used to it, the better. All you need is a lightweight puppy collar; you can buy something more exotic when your Chihuahua is fully grown.

A nylon leash is suitable for early leash training, but make sure the fastening is secure. Again, you can invest in a more expensive leash at a later date – there are lots of attractive collar and leash sets to choose from.

ID

Your Chihuahua needs to wear some form of ID when he is out in public places. This can be in form of a disc, engraved with your contact details, attached to the collar. When your Chi is full-grown, you can buy an embroidered collar with your contact details, which eliminates the danger of the disc becoming detached from the collar.

You may also wish to consider a permanent form of ID. Increasingly, breeders are getting puppies micro-chipped before they go to their new homes. A micro-chip is the size of a grain of rice. It is 'injected' under the skin, usually between the shoulder blades, with a special needle. It has some tiny barbs on it, which dig into the tissue around where it lies, so it does not migrate from that spot.

Each chip has its own unique identification number, which can only be read by a special scanner. That ID number is then registered on a national database with your name and details, so that if ever your dog is lost, he can be taken to any vet or rescue centre where he is scanned and then you are contacted.

If your puppy has not been micro-chipped, you can ask your vet to do it, maybe when he goes along for his vaccinations.

Bowls

Your Chihuahua will need two bowls – one for food, and one for fresh drinking water, which should always be readily available. A stainless steel bowl is a good choice for a food bowl as it is tough and hygienic. Plastic bowls may be chewed, and there is a danger that bacteria can collect in the small cracks that may appear.

You can opt for a second stainless steel bowl for drinking water, or you may prefer a heavier ceramic bowl which will not be knocked over so easily.

Many breeders have puppies microchipped before they go to their new homes.

Food

The breeder will let you know what your puppy is eating and should provide a full diet sheet to guide you through the first six months of your puppy's feeding regime – how much they are eating per meal, how many meals per day, when to increase the amounts given per meal and when to reduce the meals per day.

The breeder may provide you with some food when you collect your puppy, but it is worth making enquiries in advance about the availability of the brand that is recommended.

Grooming equipment

A smooth-coat puppy will need minimal coat care, but it is important that he gets used to being handled from an early age. Buy a soft, natural bristle brush and accustom your pup to short grooming sessions.

A long-coated pup will need more attention. For this coat type you need a hard bristle brush and a metal comb.

Both varieties require:

- Guillotine nail clippers
- Toothbrush (a finger brush is easiest to use) and specially-manufactured dog toothpaste

- Cotton (cotton-wool) pads for cleaning the eyes and ears

Toys must be sufficiently robust to withstand chewing.

Toys

The Chihuahua loves his toys, and it seems that most dogs have their personal favourites. Some like soft types, some prefer hard, rubber toys they can chew, and others enjoy the boredom busters that can be filled with treats. The best plan is to buy a small selection and find out which type your Chi likes best.

Your guiding principle when choosing a toy must be whether it is suitably robust, as a Chi can be surprisingly destructive. You should also get into the habit of checking toys on a regular basis for signs of wear and tear. If your puppy swallows a chunk of rubber or plastic, it could cause an internal blockage. This could involve costly surgery to remove the offending item, or at worst, it could prove fatal.

Finding a vet

Before your puppy arrives home, you should register with a vet. Visit some the vets in your local area, and seek a recommendation from other pet owners. It is so important to find a good vet, almost as much as finding a good doctor for yourself. You need someone you can build a good rapport with and have complete faith in. Word of mouth is really the best recommendation.

When you contact a veterinary practice, find out the following:

- Does the surgery run an appointment system?

- What are the arrangements for emergency, out of hours cover?

- Do any of the vets in the practice have experience treating Chihuahuas?

- What facilities are available at the practice?

If you are satisfied with what your find, and the staff appear to be helpful and friendly, book an appointment so your puppy can have a health check a couple of days after you collect him.

Facing page: Find a veterinary practice that has experience in treating Chihuahuas.

Settling in

When you first arrive home with your puppy, be careful not to overwhelm him. You and your family are hugely excited, but the puppy is in a completely strange environment with new sounds, smells and sights, which is a daunting experience, even for the boldest of pups.

Some puppies are very confident, wanting to play straightaway and quickly making friends; others need a little longer. Keep a close check on your Chihuahua's body language and reactions so you can proceed at a pace he is comfortable with.

First, let him explore the garden. He will probably need to relieve himself after the journey home, so take him to the allocated toileting area and, when he performs, give him plenty of praise.

When you take your puppy indoors, let him investigate again. Show him his crate, and encourage him to go in by throwing in a treat. Let him have a sniff, and allow him to go in and out as he

pleases. Later on, when he is tired, you can put him in the crate while you stay in the room. In this way he will learns to settle and will not think he is being abandoned.

It is a good idea to feed your puppy in his crate, at least to begin with, as this helps to build up a positive association. It will not be long before your Chihuahua sees his crate as his own special den and will go there as a matter of choice. Some owners place a blanket over the crate, covering the back and sides, so that it is even more cosy and den-like.

Meeting the family

Resist the temptation of inviting friends and neighbors to come and meet the new arrival; your puppy needs to focus on getting to know his new family for the first few days. Try not to swamp your Chihuahua with too much attention; give him a chance to explore and find his feet. There will be plenty of time for cuddles later on!

If you have children in the family, you need to keep everything as calm as possible. Your puppy may not have met children before, and, even if he has, he will still find them strange and unpredictable. A puppy can easily become alarmed by too much noise, or he may go to the opposite extreme and become over-excited, which can lead to mouthing and nipping.

The best plan is to get the children to sit on the floor and give them all a treat. Each child can then call the puppy, stroke him, and offer a treat. In this way the puppy is making the decisions rather than being forced into interactions he may find stressful.

If he tries to nip or mouth, make sure there is a toy at the ready, so his attention can be diverted to something he is allowed to bite. If you do this consistently, he will learn to inhibit his desire to mouth when he is interacting with people.

Right from the start, impose a rule that the children are not allowed to pick up or carry the puppy. They can cuddle him when they are sitting on the floor. This may sound a little severe, but a wriggly puppy can be dropped in an instant, sometimes with disastrous consequences.

Involve all family members with the day-to-day care of your puppy; this will enable the bond to develop with the whole family as opposed to just one person. Encourage the children to train and reward the puppy, teaching him to follow their commands without question.

The animal family

Chihuahuas enjoy the company of other dogs, particularly their own kind. But regardless of breed, you will need to supervise early interactions so relations with the resident dog get off on a good footing. A Chihuahua will not be daunted by the sight of a larger dog, so you need to ensure that a sense of mutual respect is established.

Your adult dog may be allowed to meet the puppy at the home of the breeder. This is ideal as the older dog will not feel threatened if he is away from home. But if this is not possible, allow your dog to smell the puppy's bedding (the bedding supplied by the breeder is fine) before they actually meet, so he familiarizes himself with the puppy's scent.

The garden is the best place for introducing the puppy, as the adult will regard it as neutral territory. He will probably take a great interest in the puppy and sniff him all over. Most puppies are naturally submissive in this situation, and your pup may lick the other dog's mouth or roll over on to his back. Try not to interfere as this is the natural way that dogs get to know each other.

You will only need to intervene if the older dog is too boisterous, and alarms the puppy. In this case, it is a good idea to put the adult on a leash so you have some measure of control.

It rarely takes long for an adult to accept a puppy, particularly if you make a big fuss of the older dog so that he still feels special. However, do not take any risks, and supervise all interactions for the first few weeks. If you do need to leave the dogs alone, always make sure your puppy is safe in his crate.

Meeting a cat should be supervised in a similar way, but do not allow your puppy to chase the cat, as it may well retaliate, using its sharp claws. The best plan is to hold your puppy, and distract his attention with treats so that he does not become too obsessed. If you repeat this a few times, praising your puppy when he focuses on you, he will realize that you are more interesting than the cat, and the novelty of having a cat in the home will soon wear off.

Generally, the Chihuahua-feline relationship should not cause any serious problems. Indeed, many Chihuahuas count the family cat among their best friends!

Feeding

The breeder will generally provide enough food for the first few days so the puppy does not have to cope with a change in diet – and possible digestive upset – along with all the stress of moving home.

Some puppies polish off their food from the first meal onwards, others are more concerned by their new surroundings and are too distracted to eat. Do not worry unduly if your puppy seems disinterested in his food for the first day or so. Give him 10 minutes to eat what he wants and then remove the leftovers and start afresh at the next meal.

Do not make the mistake of trying to tempt his appetite with tasty treats or you will end up with a faddy feeder. This is a mistake made by all too many Chi owners, and a scenario can develop where the dog holds out, refusing to eat his food, in the hope that something better will be offered.

Obviously if you have any concerns about your puppy in the first few days, seek advice from your vet.

The first night

Your puppy will have spent the first weeks of his life with his mother or curled up with his siblings. He is then taken from everything he knows as familiar, lavished with attention by his new family – and then comes bed time when he is left all alone. It is little wonder that he feels abandoned.

The best plan is to establish a night-time routine, and then stick to it so that your puppy knows what is expected of him. Take your puppy out into the garden to relieve himself, and then settle him in his crate. Some people leave a low light on for the puppy at night for the first week, others have tried a radio as company or a ticking clock. A covered hot-water bottle, filled with warm water, can also be a comfort. Like people, puppies are individuals and what works for one does not necessarily work for another, so it is a matter of trial and error.

Be very positive when you leave your puppy on his own; do not linger, or keep returning; this will make the situation more difficult. It is inevitable that he will protest to begin with, but if you stick to your routine, he will accept that he gets left at night – and you always return in the morning.

Rescued dogs

Settling an older, rescued dog in the home is very similar to a puppy in as much as you will need to make the same preparations regarding his homecoming. As with a puppy, an older dog will need you to be consistent, so start as you mean to go on.

There is often an initial honeymoon period when you bring a rescued dog home, where he will be on his best behavior for the first few weeks. It is after these first couple of weeks that the true nature of the dog will show, so be prepared for subtle changes in his behavior. It may be advisable to register with a reputable training club, so you can seek advice on any training or behavioural issues at an early stage.

Above all, remember that a rescued dog ceases to be a rescued dog the moment he enters his forever home and should be treated normally like any other family dog.

Facing page: A rescued dog needs special consideration as he settles in a new home.

House training

This is an aspect of training that most first-time puppy owners dread, but it should not be a problem as along as you are prepared to put in the time and effort.

Some breeders start the house-training process by providing the litter with paper or training pads so they learn to keep their sleeping quarters clean. This is a step in the right direction, but most pet owners want their puppies to toilet outside.

As discussed earlier, you will have allocated a toileting area in your garden when preparing for your puppy's homecoming. You need to take your puppy to this area every time he needs to relieve himself so he builds up an association and knows why you have brought him out to the garden.

Establish a routine and make sure you take your puppy out at the following times:

- First thing in the morning

- After mealtimes

- On waking

- Following a play session

- Last thing at night.

A puppy should be taken out to relieve himself every two hours as an absolute minimum. If you can manage an hourly trip out, so much the better. The more often your puppy gets it 'right', the quicker he will learn to be clean in the house. It helps if you use a verbal cue, such as "Busy", when your pup is performing and, in time, this will trigger the desired response.

Do not be tempted to put your puppy out on the doorstep in the hope that he will toilet on his own. Most pups simply sit there, waiting to get back inside the house! No matter how bad the weather is, accompany your puppy and give him lots of praise when he performs correctly.

Do not rush back inside as soon as he has finished, your puppy might start to delay in the hope of prolonging his time outside with you. Praise him, have a quick game – and then you can both return indoors.

When accidents happen

No matter how vigilant you are, there are bound to be accidents. If you witness the accident, take your puppy outside immediately, and give him lots of praise if he finishes his business out there.

If you are not there when he has an accident, do not scold him when you discover what has happened. He will not remember what he has done and will not understand why you are cross with him. Simply clean it up and resolve to be more vigilant next time.

Make sure you use a deodorizer (available in pet stores) when you clean up, otherwise your pup will be drawn to the smell and may be tempted to use the same spot again.

Choosing a diet

There are so many different types of dog food on sale – all claiming to be the best – so how do you know what is likely to suit your Chihuahua? He may be small in size, but he is high in energy and needs a well balanced diet that is suited to his individual requirements.

When choosing a diet, there are basically three categories to choose from:

Complete

This is probably the most popular diet, as it is easy to feed and is specially formulated with all the nutrients your dog needs. This means that you should not add any supplements or you may upset the nutritional balance.

Most complete diets come in different life stages – puppy, adult maintenance and senior – so this means that your Chihuahua is getting what he needs when he is growing, during adulthood, and as he becomes older. You can even get prescription diets for dogs with particular health issues.

There are many different brands to choose from, so it is advisable to seek advice from your puppy's breeder, who will have lengthy experience of feeding Chihuahuas.

Canned/pouches

This type of food is usually fed with hard biscuit, and most Chihuahuas find it very appetizing. However, the ingredients – and the nutritional value – does vary significantly between the different brands so you will need to check the label. This type of food often has a high moisture content, so you need to be sure your Chihuahua is getting all the nutrition he needs.

A Chi puppy needs four small meals, evenly spaced throughout the day.

Homemade

Some owners like to prepare meals especially for their dogs – and it is probably much appreciated. The danger is that although the food is tasty, and your Chi may appreciate the variety, you cannot be sure that it has the correct nutritional balance.

If this is a route you want to go down, you will need to find out the exact ratio of fats, carbohydrates, proteins, minerals and vitamins that are needed, which is quite an undertaking.

The Barf (Biologically Appropriate Raw Food) diet is another, more natural approach to feeding.

Dogs are fed a diet mimicking what they would have eaten in the wild, consisting of raw meat, bone, muscle, fat, and vegetable matter. Some owners worry that small breeds cannot cope with this diet, but there is evidence that they do well on it, particularly as many small dogs are prone to dental problems. The best plan is to seek advice from your vet.

Feeding regime

When your puppy arrives in his new home he will need four meals, evenly spaced throughout the day. You may decide to keep to the diet recommended by your puppy's breeder, and if your pup is thriving there is no need to change. However, if your puppy is not doing well on the food, or you have problems with supply, you will need to make a change.

When switching diets, it is very important to do it on a gradual basis, changing over from one food to the next, a little at a time, and spreading the transition over a week to 10 days. This will avoid the risk of digestive upset.

When your puppy is around 12 weeks, you can cut out one of his meals; he may well have started to leave some of his food indicating he is ready to do this. By six months, he can move on to two meals a day – a regime that will suit him for the rest of his life.

Bones and chews

Puppies love to chew, and many adults also enjoy gnawing on a bone. Bones should always be hard and uncooked; rib bones and poultry bones must be avoided as they can splinter and cause major problems. Dental chews, and some of the manufactured rawhide chews are safe, but they should only be given under supervision.

Ideal weight

Obesity is one of the major health issues in the breed, and there is only one person to blame – the over-indulgent owner. It is your responsibility to feed a well balanced diet, and to keep a close check on your Chihuahua's weight.

Most adults thrive on a regime of two meals a day.

Unfortunately, the Chihuahua has perfected the art of looking at your with his melting dark eyes, and telling you he is 'starving', which can be very hard to resist. But you will need to harden your heart and think of your dog's figure! With a small breed, it is so easy for the pounds to pile on, so monitor everything he eats.

If you are using treats for training, remember to take these into calculation and reduce the amount you feed at his next meal. You can also give your Chi healthy treats, such as a slice of carrot or apple, which will exercise his teeth and jaws.

Some owners find it difficult to judge whether a dog is the correct weight. A good guide is to look at your Chihuahua from above, and make sure you can see a definite 'waist', just behind the ribcage. You should be able to feel his ribs, but not see them.

In order to keep a close check on your Chihuahua's weight, get into the habit of visiting your veterinary surgery on a monthly basis so that you can weigh him. You can keep a record of his weight so you can make adjustments if necessary.

If you are concerned that your Chi is putting on too much weight, consult your vet, who will help you to plan a suitable diet.

Facing page: It is your responsibility to keep your Chihuahua at the correct weight.

Caring for your Chihuahua

The Chihuahua does not demand a lot from his owners. But like all living creatures, he has his own special needs, which you should be aware of.

Puppy grooming

The amount of grooming required depends on whether you have a smooth-coated or long-coated Chihuahua. In fact, a long-coated puppy will not have much in the way of feathering until his adult coat comes through, but he needs to get used to regular grooming sessions.

First, teach your puppy to stand on a table. It does not have to be a purpose-built grooming table – just one that is steady and is the right height for you to

attend to your Chi without getting backache. Place a rubber mat on the table so your puppy does not slip and, to start with, let him sit or stand while you stroke him, and praise him for being calm. Reward him with a treat, and that will be sufficient for the first session.

The next day, you can start grooming; just a few strokes with a natural bristle brush for a smooth coat, and the same attention for a long coat, only you will need to use a hard bristle brush. Hopefully, the breeder will have started grooming lessons, so once your puppy feels confident with you, he should start to relax.

Gradually increase the amount of time you can spend grooming your puppy, and, with a long coat, start to work through his coat, very gently, with a metal comb.

Adult grooming

If you have accustomed your Chihuahua to being handled from an early age, he will positively enjoy his grooming sessions. Bear in mind that even if a smooth-coat looks in good order, the process of grooming acts as a massage and aids circulation.

When the adult coat comes through, the smooth may or may not have an undercoat. The topcoat is close-fitting and there is more fur around the ruff and on the tail, often referred to as a 'beaver' tail. Regular brushing with a soft bristle brush is all that is required. When the coat is shedding, you may find a small pin brush helps to remove the dead hair.

The long-coated Chihuahua needs regular grooming as his coat will mat and tangle if it is neglected. Use a hard bristle brush to work through the coat, and then follow this up by combing it through. Be careful to tease out tangles, rather than pulling at them, which will be painful for your Chihuahua. A bad experience can cause problems in the future, so make sure grooming sessions are positive, giving your Chi the occasional treat when he co-operates so he learns to accept, and enjoy, the procedure.

Bathing

As the Chihuahua is so small, you can bath him in the sink, but you do not need to do this very often as bathing destroys the natural oils in the coat. However, there will be times when your Chi has rolled in something smelly, or when there is a build up of doggy odor, and bathing is the only option.

If you have a long-coat, remember to groom before bathing, making sure the coat is free from mats and tangles. You will need to use a shampoo specifically for dogs, and only use a conditioner now and again. It is essential that all traces of shampoo and conditioner are rinsed from the coat as any residue could trigger a skin irritation.

Routine care

In addition to grooming, you will need to carry out some routine care.

Eyes

Check the eyes for signs of soreness or discharge. You can use a piece of cotton (cotton-wool) – a separate piece for each eye – and wipe away any debris.

Ears

The ears should be clean and free from odor. You can buy specially manufactured ear wipes, or you can use a piece of cotton to clean them if necessary. Do not probe into the ear canal or you risk doing more harm than good.

With long-coated Chihuahuas, you will also need to pluck the hair that grows inside the ear. This is most easily done using finger and thumb. Start doing this from an early age, rewarding your puppy for his co-operation, so he learns to accept it without a fuss. It helps if you wear rubber gloves for this job, and you can also use a powder, which helps you to grip the hair more easily.

A 'polish' with a chamois leather will keep the smooth-coat in good order.

A bristle brush is needed for the long-coated Chi.

Combing will prevent mats and tangles.

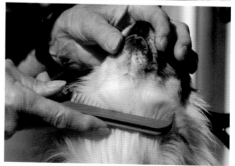

Teeth

Dental disease is becoming more prevalent among dogs so teeth cleaning should be seen as an essential part of your care regime. This applies most particularly to Toy breeds, which tend to have more problems with their teeth. The build up of tartar on the teeth can result in tooth decay, gum infection and bad breath, and if it is allowed to accumulate, you may have no option but to get the teeth cleaned under anesthetic.

When your Chihuahua is still a puppy, accustom him to teeth cleaning so it becomes a matter of routine. Dog toothpaste comes in a variety of meaty flavours, which your Chi will like, so you can start by putting some toothpaste on your finger and gently rubbing his teeth. You can then progress to using a finger brush or a toothbrush, whichever you find most convenient.

Remember to reward your Chihuahua when he co-operates and then he will positively look forward to his teeth-cleaning sessions.

Feet

Nail trimming is a task dreaded by many owners – and many dogs – but, again, if you start early on, your Chihuahua will get used to the procedure.

The ears should be clean and odor-free.

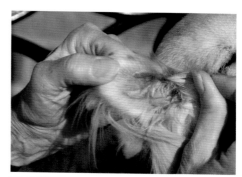

Accustom your Chi to having his teeth checked.

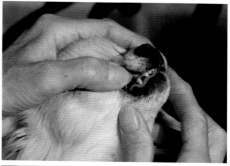

With practice, your Chi will learn to relax when his nails are being trimmed.

Nails may be dark-colored or white. Dark nails are harder to trim as you cannot see the quick (the vein that runs through the nail), which will bleed if it is nicked. The best policy is to trim little and often, so the nails don't grow too long, and you do not risk cutting too much and catching the quick.

If you are worried about trimming your Chihuahua's nails, go to your vet so you can see it done properly. If you are still concerned, you can always use the services of a professional groomer.

With a long-coated Chihuahua, you will need to trim hair that grows between the pads. If this grows too long, it becomes matted and can cause lameness. You can also trim the hair around the foot to give a neat finish.

Exercise

The Chihuahua does not need lots of exercise, which is why he is suitable for people getting on in years or for those with disabilities. He will enjoy pottering around in the garden, but you should also give him the opportunity to explore new places. Going for walks, no matter how short they are, allows a dog to use his nose and to investigate new sights and smells, which will provide mental stimulation.

If you are a keen walker, the Chihuahua will be happy

Facing page: Not for every Chi, but swimming is an excellent form of exercise.

to accompany you, and he can cover reasonable distances. The key is to build up this exercise gradually so your Chihuahua develops the muscles and the stamina to cope with this degree of physical exertion.

The older Chihuahua

We are fortunate the Chihuahua has a very good life expectancy, and you will not notice any significant changes in your dog until he reaches double figures, or even beyond.

The older Chi will sleep more, and he may be reluctant to go for longer walks. He may show signs of stiffness when he gets up from his bed, but these generally ease when he starts moving. Some older Chihuahuas may have impaired vision, and some may become a little deaf, but as long as their senses do not deteriorate dramatically, this is something older dogs learn to live with.

If you treat your older Chi with kindness and consideration, he will enjoy his later years and suffer the minimum of discomfort. It is advisable to switch him over to a senior diet, which is more suited to his needs, and you may need to adjust the quantity, as he will not be burning up the calories as he did when he was younger and more energetic. Make sure his sleeping quarters are warm and free from

Facing page: The older Chi deserves special consideration.

drafts, and if he gets wet, make sure you dry him thoroughly.

Most important of all, be guided by your Chihuahua. He will have good days when he feels up to going for a walk, and other days when he would prefer to potter in the garden. If you have a younger dog at home, this may well stimulate your Chi to take more of an interest in what is going on, but make sure he is not pestered as he needs to rest undisturbed when he is tired.

Letting go

Inevitably there comes a time when your Chihuahua is not enjoying a good quality of life, and you need to make the painful decision to let him go. We would all wish that our dogs died, painlessly, in their sleep but, unfortunately, this is rarely the case.

However, we can allow our dogs to die with dignity, and to suffer as a little as possible, and this should be our way of saying thank you for the wonderful companionship they have given us.

When you feel the time is drawing close, talk to your vet who will be able to make an objective assessment of your Chihuahua's condition and will help you to make the right decision.

This is the hardest thing you will ever have to do

as a dog owner, and it is only natural to grieve for your beloved Chi. But eventually, you will be able to look back on the happy memories of times spent together, and this will bring much comfort. You may, in time, feel that your life is not complete without a Chihuahua, and you will feel ready to welcome a new puppy into your home.

Social skills

To live in the modern world, without fears and anxieties, a Chihuahua needs to receive an education in social skills so that he learns to cope calmly and confidently in a wide variety of situations. This is important for all breeds, but it is vital for a Chihuahua, a tiny animal in a big world.

Early learning

The breeder will have started a program of socialization by getting the puppies used to all the sights and sounds of a busy household. You need to continue this when your pup arrives in his new home, making sure he is not worried by household equipment, such the vacuum cleaner or the washing machine, and that he gets used to unexpected noises from the radio and television.

As already highlighted, it is important that you handle your puppy on a regular basis

so he will accept grooming and other routine care, and will not be worried if he has to be examined by your vet.

To begin with, your puppy needs to get used to all the members of his new family, but then you should give him the opportunity to meet friends and other people who come to the house. The Chihuahua likes to make his presence felt; a warning bark is acceptable, but you do not want a dog who will not stop barking. It is therefore important to establish good greeting manners from an early age.

When your puppy has said his first 'hello', distract his attention by calling him to you and giving him a treat. You can also give the visitor a couple of treats so that when your puppy approaches – and is not barking – he can be rewarded. This may take a bit of practice, but it is well worth persevering.

If you do not have children, make sure your puppy has the chance to meet and play with other people's children so he learns that humans come in small sizes, too.

The outside world

When your puppy has completed his vaccinations, he is ready to venture into the outside world. Chihuahua puppies take a lively interest in anything new and will relish the opportunity to broaden their horizons.

However, there is a lot for a small puppy to take on board, so do not swamp him with too many new experiences when you first set out.

The best plan is to start in a quiet area with light traffic, and only progress to a busier place when your puppy is ready. There is so much to see and hear – people (maybe carrying bags or umbrellas), pushchairs, bicycles, cars, trucks, machinery – so give your puppy a chance to take it all in.

If he does appear worried, do not fall into the trap of sympathizing with him, or worse still, picking him up. This will only teach your pup that he had a good reason to be worried and, with luck, you will 'rescue' him if he feels scared.

Instead, give him a little space so he does not have to confront whatever he is frightened of, and distract him with a few treats. Then encourage him to walk past, using a calm, no-nonsense approach. Your pup will take the lead from you, and will realize there is nothing to fear.

Your pup must also continue his education in canine manners, started by his mother and by his littermates, as he needs to be able to greet all dogs calmly, giving the signals that say he is friendly and offers no threat. If you have a friend who has a dog of sound temperament, this is an ideal beginning. As your puppy gets older and more established, you can widen his circle of canine acquaintances.

Training classes

A training class will give your Chihuahua the opportunity to interact with other dogs, and he will also learn to focus on you in a different, distracting environment.

But with a tiny Chi, you must make absolutely sure that the classes are well run or you will do more damage than good. A boisterous pup can bowl a tiny Chi over in a split second. This is potentially dangerous, but it may also be traumatic and have significance on all future encounters with dogs.

Before you sign up for classes, attend a class as an observer to make sure you are happy with what goes on.

Find out the following:

- How much training experience do the instructors have?

- Are the classes divided into appropriate age categories?

- Do the instructors have experience training Toy dogs?

- Do they use positive, reward-based training methods?

If the training class is well run, it is certainly worth attending. Both you and your Chihuahua will learn useful training exercises; it will increase his social skills, and you will have the chance to talk to lots of like-minded dog enthusiasts.

Training guidelines

We are fortunate that the Chihuahua is a highly intelligent dog and is quick to learn. However, he also has a mind of his own and, given the opportunity, he will run rings around you. You need to earn his respect so he is willing to co-operate with you.

You may be keen to get started, but in your rush to get training underway, do not neglect the fundamentals that could make the difference between success and failure.

When you start training, try to observe the following guidelines:

- Choose an area that is free from distractions so your puppy will focus on you. You can move on to a more challenging environment as your pup progresses.

- Do not train your puppy just after he has eaten or when you have returned from exercise. He will either be too full, or too tired, to concentrate.

- Do not train if you are in a bad mood, or if you are short of time – these sessions always end in disaster!

- Make sure you have a reward your Chihuahua values – tasty treats, such as cheese or cooked liver, or an extra special toy.

- If you are using treats, make sure they are bite-size, otherwise you will lose momentum when your pup stops to chew on his treat.

- Keep your verbal cues simple, and always use the same one for each exercise. For example, when you ask your puppy to go into the Down position, the cue is "Down", not "Lie Down", Get Down", or anything else... Remember, your Chihuahua does not speak English; he associates the sound of the word with the action.

- If your Chi is finding an exercise difficult, break it down into small steps so it is easier to understand.

- Do not make your training sessions boring and repetitious; your Chihuahua will quickly lose interest.

- Do not train for too long, particularly with a young puppy, which will have a very short attention span, and always end training sessions on a positive note.

- Above all, have fun so you and your Chihuahua enjoy spending quality time together.

First lessons

A Chihuahua puppy will soak up new experiences like a sponge, so training should start from the time your pup arrives in his new home. It is so much easier to teach good habits rather than trying to correct your puppy when he has established an undesirable pattern of behavior.

Wearing a collar

You may, or may not, want your Chihuahua to wear a collar all the time, but when he goes out in public places he will need to be on a leash, and so he should be used to the feel of a collar around his neck. The best plan is to accustom your pup to wearing a soft collar for a few minutes at a time until he gets used to it.

Fit the collar so that you can get at least two fingers between the collar and his neck. Then have a game to distract his attention. This will work for a few moments; then he will stop, put his back leg up behind his neck, and scratch away at the peculiar itchy thing that feels so odd.

Bend down, rotate the collar, pat him on the head and distract him by playing with a toy or giving him a treat. Once he has worn the collar for a few minutes each day, he will soon become used to it and ignore it.

Remember, never leave the collar on the puppy unsupervised, especially when he is outside in the garden, or when he is in his crate, as it is could get snagged, causing serious injury.

Walking on the leash

Once your puppy is used to the collar, take him outside into your secure garden where there are no distractions.

Attach the leash and, to begin with, allow him to wander with the leash trailing, making sure it does not become snagged up. Then pick up the leash and follow the pup where he wants to go; he needs to get used to the sensation of being attached to you.

The next stage is to get your Chihuahua to follow you, and for this you will need some tasty treats. You can show him a treat in your hand, and then encourage him to follow you. Walk a few paces, and, if he is co-operating, stop and reward him. If he puts on the brakes, simply change direction and lure him with the treat.

Next, introduce some changes of direction so your puppy is walking confidently alongside you. At this stage, introduce a verbal cue "Heel" when your puppy is in the correct position. You can then graduate to walking your puppy outside the home – as long as he has completed his vaccination program – starting in quiet areas and building up to busier environments.

Do not expect too much of your puppy too soon when you are leash walking away from home. He will be distracted by all the new sights and sounds he encounters, so concentrating on leash training will be difficult for him. Give him a chance to look and see, and reward him frequently when he is walking forward confidently on a loose leash.

Try not to get into the habit of picking your Chihuahua up if he seems reluctant to walk on his leash. You will be teaching him that the moment he gives up, you will come to the rescue rather than encouraging him to be confident standing on his own four feet.

Do not put too much pressure on your Chi to begin with.

Come when called

You may think you do not need to teach a recall to a tiny dog that is unlikely to stray. But you would be making a big mistake. The Chihuahua can move at lightning speed when something catches his attention, and a reliable recall could prove to be a lifesaver.

It is also important to remember that the Chihuahua is a dog and, as such, he likes the opportunity to explore and investigate new scents. You may not take him on lengthy treks, but you want to have the confidence to let him off leash, knowing he will return when you call him.

The breeder may have started this lesson, simply by calling the puppies to "Come" when it is a mealtime, or when they are moving from one place to another.

You can build on this when your puppy arrives in

his new home, calling him to "Come" when he is in a confined space, such as the kitchen. This is a good place to build up a positive association with the verbal cue – particularly if you ask your puppy to "Come" to get his dinner!

The next stage is to transfer the lesson to the garden. Arm yourself with some treats, and wait until your puppy is distracted. Then call him, using a higher-pitched, excited tone of voice. At this stage, a puppy wants to be with you, so capitalize on this and keep practicing the verbal cue, rewarding your puppy with a treat and lots of praise when he comes to you.

Now you are ready to introduce some distractions. Try calling him when someone else is in the garden, or wait a few minutes until he is investigating a really interesting scent. When he responds, make a really big fuss of him and give him some extra treats so he knows it is worth his while to come to you. If your puppy responds, immediately reward him with a treat.

If he is slow to come, run away a few steps and then call again, making yourself sound really exciting. Jump up and down, open your arms wide to welcome him; it doesn't matter how silly you look, he needs to see you as the most fun person in the world.

When you have a reliable recall in the garden, you

can venture into the outside world. Do not be too ambitious to begin with; try a recall on a quiet place with the minimum of distractions and only progress to more challenging environments if your Chihuahua is responding well.

Do not make the mistake of only asking your dog to come at the end of a walk. What is the incentive in coming back to you if all you do is clip on his lead and head for home? Instead, call your dog at random times throughout the walk, giving him a treat and a stroke, and then letting him go free again. In this way, coming to you is always rewarding, and does not signal the end of his free run.

Coming back should always be a rewarding experience.

Stationary
exercises

The Sit and Down are easy to teach, and mastering these exercises will be rewarding for both you and your Chihuahua.

Sit

The best method is to lure your Chi into position, and for this you can use a treat, a toy, or his food bowl.

- Hold the reward (a treat or food bowl) above his head. As he looks up, he will lower his hindquarters and go into a sit.

- Practice this a few times and when your puppy understands what you are asking, introduce the verbal cue "Sit".

- When your Chihuahua understands the exercise, he will respond to the verbal cue alone, and you will not need to reward him every time he sits. However, it is a good idea to give him a treat on a random basis when he co-operates to keep him guessing!

Down

This is an important lesson, which can be used in a variety of situations.

You can start with your dog in a Sit or a Stand for this exercise. Stand or kneel in front of him and show him you have a treat in your hand. Hold the treat just in front of his nose and slowly lower it towards the ground, between his front legs.

As your Chihuahua follows the treat he will go down on his front legs and, in a few moments, his hindquarters will follow. Close your hand over the treat so he doesn't cheat and get the treat before he is in the correct position. As soon as he is in the Down, give him the treat and lots of praise.

Keep practicing, and when your Chi understands what you want, introduce the verbal cue "Down".

Control exercises

These exercises are not the most exciting but they are useful in a variety of different situations. They also teach your Chihuahua that you are someone to be respected, and that he is always rewarded for making the right decision.

Wait

This exercise teaches your Chihuahua to "Wait" in position until you give the next command; it differs from the Stay exercise where he must stay where you have left him for a more prolonged period. The most useful application of "Wait" is when you are getting your dog out of the car and you need him to stay in position until you clip on his lead.

Start with your puppy on the lead to give you a greater chance of success. Ask him to "Sit" stand in front him. Step back one pace, holding your hand,

palm flat, facing him. Wait a second and then come back to stand in front of him. You can then reward him and release him with a word, such as "OK".

Practice this a few times, waiting a little longer before you reward him, and then introduce the verbal cue "Wait".

You can reinforce the lesson by using it in different situations, such as asking your Chihuahua to "Wait" before you put his food bowl down.

Stay

You need to differentiate this exercise from the Wait by using a different hand signal and a different verbal cue.

Start with your Chihuahua in the Down as he most likely to be secure in this position. Stand by his side and then step forwards, with your hand held back, palm facing the dog.

Step back, release him, and then reward him. Practice until your Chi understands the exercise and then introduce the verbal cue "Stay".

Gradually increase the distance you can leave your puppy, and increase the challenge by walking around him – and even stepping over him – so that he learns he must "Stay" until you release him.

Leave

A response to this verbal cue means that your Chihuahua will learn to give up a toy on request, and it follows on that he will give up anything when he is asked, which is very useful if he has got hold of a forbidden object. You can also use it if you catch him red-handed raiding the bin, or digging up a prized plant in the garden.

A game of swap will encourage your Chi to give up his toy on request.

Some Chihuahuas can be a little possessive over their toys, and so it is important that your puppy learns that if he gives up something, he will get a reward, which may be even better than what he already has!

- The "Leave" command can be taught quite easily when you are first playing with your puppy. As you gently, take a toy from his mouth, introduce the verbal cue, "Leave", and then praise him.

- If he is reluctant, swap the toy for another toy or a treat. This will usually do the trick.

- Do not try to pull the toy from his mouth if he refuses to give it up, as it will only make him keener to hang on to it. Let the toy go 'dead' in your hand, and then swap it for a new, exciting toy, so this becomes the better option.

- Remember to make a big fuss of your Chihuahua when he co-operates. If he is rewarded with verbal praise, plus a game with a toy or a tasty treat, he will learn that "Leave" is always a good option.

Opportunities
for Chihuahuas

If you have enjoyed training your Chihuahua, you may consider going a stage further and teaching some more advanced exercises, or getting involved in one of the many canine sports on offer. Of course, you have to be aware of the limitations imposed by the Chihuahua's size, but you will be surprised how versatile these little dogs can be.

Good Citizen Scheme

The Kennel Club Good Citizen Scheme was introduced to promote responsible dog ownership, and to teach dogs basic good manners. In the US there is one test; in the UK there are four award levels – Puppy Foundation, Bronze, Silver and Gold.

Exercises within the scheme include:

- Walking on leash

- Road walking

- Control at door/gate.

- Food manners

- Recall

- Stay

- Send to bed

- Emergency stop.

Competitive obedience

This is a sport where you are assessed as a dog and handler, completing a series of exercises including heelwork, recalls, retrieves, stays, sendaways and scent discrimination.

In the US, it is not unusual for owners of Toy dogs to compete in this discipline, and Chihuahuas and Chihuahua crosses have proved they are more than capable of making their mark.

Obedience exercises are relatively simple to begin with, involving heelwork, a recall and stays in the lowest class, and, as you progress through, more exercises are added, and the aids you are allowed to give are reduced.

To achieve top honours in this discipline requires intensive training, as precision and accuracy are of paramount importance. However, you must guard against drilling your Chihuahua, as he will quickly lose motivation.

Agility

The Chihuahua can be very speedy if he has sufficient motivation. With good training, Chihuahuas and Chihuahua crosses are can be highly successful competing in the category for small dogs.

In this sport, the dog completes an obstacle course under the guidance of his owner. You need a good element of control, as the dog competes off the leash. In competition, the dog that completes the course with the fewest faults, in the fastest time, wins the class. The obstacles include an A-frame, a dog-walk, weaving poles, a see-saw, tunnels, and jumps.

Rally O

If you do not want to get involved in the rigors of Competitive Obedience, you may find that a sport called Rally O is more to your liking.

This is loosely based on Obedience, and also has a few exercises borrowed from Agility when you get to the highest levels. Handler and dog must complete a course, in the designated order, which has a variety of up to 20 different exercises. The course is timed and the team must complete within the time limit that is set, but there are no bonus marks for speed.

Showing

Exhibiting dogs in the show ring may look easy but, in fact, it requires hard work and dedication to present a dog so that he is looking his best, and training him so that will perform in the ring. Obviously, there is considerably more work involved in preparing a long-coated Chihuahua, but both varieties need the same groundwork.

In the show ring, a Chihuahua will be subjected to a detailed examination by the judge, and so he needs to be trained to accept this somewhat invasive procedure. He must learn to pose, standing completely still for the judge's assessment, and he must also show off his movement, trotting smartly on a show leash.

A dog that does not like being handled by the judge, or one that does not move freely on the leash, is never going to win top honors, even if he is a top-quality animal. To do well in the ring, a Chihuahua must be a real showman.

In order to prepare your Chi for the busy show atmosphere, you also need to work on his socialization, and then take him to ringcraft classes so you both learn what is required in the ring.

Showing at the top level is highly addictive, so watch out; once you start, you will never have a free date in your diary!

Heelwork to music

Also known as Canine Freestyle, this activity is becoming increasingly popular. Dog and handler perform a choreographed routine to music, allowing the dog to show off an array of tricks and moves, which delight the crowd. A dancing Chihuahua presents an enchanting picture and if you can form a partnership with your Chi, you could be world-beaters!

Health care

The Chihuahua is a healthy breed and, with good routine care, a well-balanced diet, and sufficient exercise, most will experience few problems.

However, it is your responsibility to put a program of preventative health care in place – and this should start from the moment your puppy, or older dog, arrives in his new home.

Vaccinations

Dogs are subject to a number of contagious diseases. In the old days, these were killers, and resulted in heartbreak for many owners. Vaccinations have now been developed, and the occurrence of the major infectious diseases is now very rare. However, this will only remain the case if all pet owners follow a strict policy of vaccinating their dogs.

There are vaccinations available for the following diseases:

Adenovirus: (Canine Adenovirus): This affects the liver; affected dogs have a classic 'blue eye'.

Distemper: A viral disease which causes chest and gastro-intestinal damage. The brain may also be affected, leading to fits and paralysis.

Parvovirus: Causes severe gastro enteritis, and most commonly affects puppies.

Leptospirosis: This bacterial disease is carried by rats and affects many mammals, including humans. It causes liver and kidney damage.

Rabies: A virus that affects the nervous system and is invariably fatal. The first signs are abnormal behavior when the infected dog may bite another animal or a person. Paralysis and death follow. Vaccination is compulsory in most countries. In the UK, dogs traveling overseas must be vaccinated.

Kennel Cough: There are several strains of Kennel Cough, but they all result in a harsh, dry, cough. This disease is rarely fatal – in fact most dogs make a good recovery within a matter of weeks and show few signs of ill health while they are affected. However, kennel cough is highly infectious among dogs that live together so, for this reason, most boarding kennels will insist that your dog is protected by the vaccine, which is given as nose drops.

Lyme Disease: This is a bacterial disease transmitted by ticks (see page 166). The first signs are limping, but the heart, kidneys and nervous system can also be affected. The ticks that transmit the disease occur in specific regions, such as the north-east states of the USA, some of the southern states, California and the upper Mississippi region. Lyme disease is still rare in the UK so vaccinations are not routinely offered.

Vaccination program

In the USA, the American Animal Hospital Association advises vaccination for core diseases, which they list as: distemper, adenovirus, parvovirus and rabies. The requirement for vaccinating for non-core diseases – leptospriosis, lyme disease and kennel cough – should be assessed depending on a dog's individual risk and his likely exposure to the disease.

In the UK, vaccinations are routinely given for distemper, adenovirus, leptospirosis and parvovirus.

In most cases, a puppy will start his vaccinations at around eight weeks of age, with the second part given a fortnight later. However, this does vary depending on the individual policy of veterinary practices, and the incidence of disease in your area.

You should also talk to your vet about whether to give annual booster vaccinations. This depends on an individual dog's levels of immunity, and how long a particular vaccine remains effective.

Parasites

No matter how well you look after your Chihuahua, you will have to accept that parasites – internal and external – are ever present, and you need to take preventative action.

Internal parasites: As the name suggests, these parasites live inside your dog. Most will find a home in the digestive tract, but there is also a parasite that lives in the heart. If infestation is unchecked, a dog's health will be severely jeopardized, but routine preventative treatment is simple and effective.

External parasites: These parasites live on your dog's body – in his skin and fur, and sometimes in his ears.

Roundworm

This is found in the small intestine, and signs of infestation will be a poor coat, a pot belly, diarrhoea and lethargy. Pregnant mothers should be treated, but it is almost inevitable that parasites will be passed on to the puppies. For this reason, a breeder

will start a worming program, which you will need to continue. Ask your vet for advice on treatment, which will need to continue throughout your dog's life.

Tapeworm

Infection occurs when fleas and lice are ingested. The adult worm takes up residence in the small intestine, releasing mobile segments (which contain eggs) that can be seen in a dog's feces as small rice-like grains. The only other obvious sign of infestation is irritation of the anus. Again, routine preventative treatment is required throughout your Chihuahua's life.

Heartworm

This parasite is transmitted by mosquitoes, and so will only occur where these insects thrive. A warm environment is needed for the parasite to develop, so it is more likely to be present in areas with a warm, humid climate. However, it is found in all parts of the USA, although its prevalence does vary. At present, heartworm is rarely seen in the UK.

Heartworm live in the right side of the heart. Larvae can grow up to 14 inches (35cm) in length. A dog with heartworm is at severe risk from heart failure, so preventative treatment, as advised by your vet, is essential. Dogs living in the USA should have regular blood tests to check for the presence of infection.

Lungworm

Lungworm, or *Angiostrongylus vasorum*, is a parasite that lives in the heart and major blood vessels supplying the lungs. It can cause many problems, such as breathing difficulties, blood-clotting problems, sickness and diarrhoea, seizures, and can even be fatal. The parasite is carried by slugs and snails, and the dog becomes infected when ingesting these, often accidentally when rummaging through undergrowth. Lungworm is not common, but it is on the increase and a responsible owner should be aware of it. Fortunately, it is easily preventable and even affected dogs usually make a full recovery if treated early enough. Your vet will be able to advise you on the risks in your area and what form of treatment may be required.

Fleas

A dog may carry dog fleas, cat fleas, and even human fleas. The flea stays on the dog only long enough to have a blood meal and to breed, but its presence will result in itching and scratching. If your dog has an allergy to fleas – which is usually a reaction to the flea's saliva – he will scratch himself until he is raw.

Spot-on treatment, which should be administered on a routine basis, is easy to use and highly effective on all types of fleas. You can also treat your dog with a spray or with insecticidal shampoo. Bear in mind that the whole environment your dog lives in will need to be sprayed, and all other pets living in your home will also need to be treated.

How to detect fleas

You may suspect your dog has fleas, but how can you be sure? There are two methods to try.

Run a fine comb through your dog's coat, and see if you can detect the presence of fleas on the skin, or clinging to the comb. Alternatively, sit your dog on white paper and rub his back. This will dislodge feces from the fleas, which will be visible as small brown specks. To double check, shake the specks on to some damp cotton (cotton-wool). Flea feces consists of the dried blood taken from the host, so if the specks turn a lighter shade of red, you know your dog has fleas.

Ticks

These are blood-sucking parasites which are most frequently found in rural areas where sheep or deer are present. The main danger is their ability to pass lyme disease to both dogs and humans. Lyme disease is prevalent in some areas of the USA (see page 161), although it is still rare in the UK.

The treatment you give your dog for fleas generally works for ticks, but you should discuss the best product to use with your vet.

How to remove a tick

If you spot a tick on your dog, do not try to pluck it off as you risk leaving the hard mouth parts embedded in his skin. The best way to remove a tick is to use a fine pair of tweezers or you can buy a tick remover. Grasp the tick head firmly and then pull the tick straight out from the skin. If you are using a tick remover, check the instructions, as some recommend a circular twist when pulling. When you have removed the tick, clean the area with mild soap and water.

Ear mites

These parasites live in the outer ear canal. The signs of infestation are a brown, waxy discharge, and your dog will continually shake his head and scratch his ear. If you suspect your Chihuahua has ear mites, a visit to the vet will be need so that medicated ear drops can be prescribed.

Fur mites

These small, white parasites are visible to the naked

eye and are often referred to as 'walking dandruff'.
They cause a scurfy coat and mild itchiness.
However, they are zoonetic – transferable to humans
– so prompt treatment with an insecticide prescribed
by your vet is essential.

Harvest mites

These are picked up from the undergrowth, and
can be seen as a bright orange patch on the
webbing between the toes, although this can be
found elsewhere on the body, such as on the ears
flaps. Treatment is effective with the appropriate
insecticide.

Skin mites

There are two types of parasite that burrow into
a dog's skin. *Demodex canis* is transferred from
a mother to her pups while they are feeding.
Treatment is with a topical preparation, and
sometimes antibiotics are needed.

The other skin mite is *Sarcoptes scabiei*, which
causes intense itching and hair loss. It is highly
contagious, so all dogs in a household will need to
be treated, which involves repeated bathing with a
medicated shampoo.

Common
ailments

As with all living animals, dogs can be affected by a variety of ailments. Most can be treated effectively after consulting with your vet, who will prescribe appropriate medication and will advise on care.

Here are some of the more common problems that could affect your Chihuahua, with advice on how to deal with them.

Anal glands

These are two small sacs on either side of the anus, which produce a dark-brown secretion that dogs use when they mark their territory. The anal glands should empty every time a dog defecates but if they become blocked or impacted, a dog will experience increasing discomfort. He may nibble at his rear end, or 'scoot' his bottom along the ground to relieve the irritation.

Treatment involves a trip to the vet, who will empty the glands manually. It is important to do this without delay or infection may occur.

Dental problems

Toy dogs suffer with dental probems more than other

breeds, and so it is important to practice good dental hygiene – in the form of regular teeth cleaning – throughout your Chihuahua's life. This will do much to minimize gum infection and tooth decay. If tartar accumulates to the extent that you cannot remove it by brushing, the vet will need to intervene. In a situation such as this, an anesthetic will need to be administered so the tartar can be removed manually.

Diarrhoea

There are many reasons why a dog has diarrhoea, but most commonly it is the result of scavenging, a sudden change of diet, or an adverse reaction to a particular type of food.

If your dog is suffering from diarrhoea, the first step is to withdraw food for a day. It is important that he does not dehydrate, so make sure that fresh drinking water is available. However, drinking too much can increase the diarrhoea, which may be accompanied with vomiting, so limit how much he drinks at any one time.

After allowing the stomach to rest, feed a bland diet, such as white fish or chicken with boiled rice, for a few days. In most cases, your dog's motions will return to normal and you can resume feeding as usual, although this should be done gradually.

However, if this fails to work and the diarrhoea persists for more than a few days, you should consult you vet. Your dog may have an infection which needs to be treated with antibiotics, or the diarrhoea may indicate some other problem which needs expert diagnosis.

Ear infections

The Chihuahua has prick ears, which allow the air to circulate; this means that there is reduced risk of ear infections. However, you should get into the habit of checking your Chi's ears on a regular basis.

A healthy ear is clean with no sign of redness or inflammation, and no evidence of a waxy brown discharge or a foul odor. If you see your dog scratching his ear, shaking his head, or holding one ear at an odd angle, you will need to consult your vet.

The most likely causes are ear mites, an infection, or there may a foreign body, such as a grass seed, trapped in the ear.

Depending on the cause, treatment is with medicated ear drops, possibly containing antibiotics. If a foreign body is suspected, the vet will need to carry our further investigations.

Eye problems

The Chihuahua's large round eyes are a feature and contribute to the saucy expression that is so typical of the breed. However, they should not protrude. This is important as breeds with prominent eyes, such as the Pekingese, are vulnerable to injury.

If your Chihuahua's eyes look red and sore, he may be suffering from conjunctivitis. This is sometimes accompanied by a watery or a crusty discharge. Conjunctivitis can be caused by a bacterial or viral infection, it could be the result of an injury, or it could be an adverse reaction to pollen.

You will need to consult your vet for a correct diagnosis, but in the case of an infection, treatment with medicated eye drops is effective.

Conjunctivitis may also be the first sign of a more serious inherited eye problem (see page 184).

In some instances, a dog may suffer from dry, itchy eye, which your dog may further injure through scratching. This condition, known as keratoconjunctivitis sicca, may be inherited.

Foreign bodies

In the home, puppies – and some older dogs – cannot resist chewing anything that looks interesting. The toys you choose for your dog should be suitably robust to withstand damage, but children's toys can be irresistible. Some dogs will chew – and swallow – anything from socks, tights, and any other items from the laundry basket to stones from the garden. Obviously, these items are indigestible and could cause an obstruction in your dog's intestine, which is potentially lethal.

The signs to look for are vomiting, and a tucked up posture. The dog will often be restless and will look as though he is in pain.

In this situation, you must get your dog to the vet without delay as surgery will be needed to remove the obstruction.

Heatstroke

The Chihuahua loves to sunbathe, particularly the smooth-coat, but you need to make sure your Chi does not overdo it. Dogs can overheat very easily on hot days, and this can have disastrous consequences. If the weather is warm make sure your Chihuahua always has access to shady areas, and wait for a cooler part of the day before going for a walk. Be extra careful if you leave your Chihuahua in the car, as the temperature can rise dramatically - even on a cloudy day. Heatstroke can happen very rapidly, and, unless you are able lower your dog's temperature, it can be fatal.

If your Chihuahua appears to be suffering from heatstroke, lie him flat and work at lowering his temperature by spraying him with cool water and covering him with a wet towel. As soon as he has made some recovery, take him to the vet where cold intravenous fluids can be administered.

Lameness/limping

There are a wide variety of reasons why a dog can go lame, from a simple muscle strain to a fracture, ligament damage, or more complex problems with the joints which may be an inherited disorder (see page 186). It takes an expert to make a correct diagnosis, so if you are concerned about your dog, do not delay in seeking help.

As your Chihuahua becomes more elderly, he may suffer from arthritis, which you will see as general stiffness, particularly when he gets up after resting. It will help if you ensure his bed is in a warm draught-free location, and if your Chihuahua gets wet after exercise, you must dry him thoroughly.

If you Chihuahua seems to be in pain, consult your vet who will be able to help with pain relief medication.

Skin problems

If your dog is scratching or nibbling at his skin, first check he is free from fleas (see page 165). There are other external parasites that cause itching and hair loss, but you will need a vet to help you find the culprit.

An allergic reaction is another major cause of skin problems. It can be quite an undertaking to find the cause of the allergy, and you will need to follow your vet's advice, which often requires eliminating specific ingredients from the diet, as well as looking at environmental factors.

Alopecia (baldness) may be a issue with some Chihuahuas; this condition may have an hereditary link (see Color Dilution Alopecia, page 184).

Breed-specific disorders

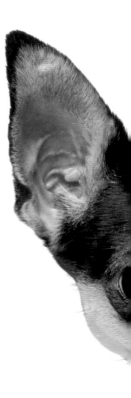

Like all pedigree dogs, the Chihuahua does have a few breed-related disorders. If diagnosed with any of the diseases listed below, it is important to remember that they can affect offspring so breeding from affected dogs should be discouraged.

There are now recognised screening tests to enable breeders to check for affected individuals and hence reduce the prevalence of these diseases within the breed.

DNA testing is also becoming more widely available, and as research into the different genetic diseases progresses, more DNA tests are being developed.

Alopecia

There are two types of alopecia that can affect Chihuahuas:

Colour Dilution Alopecia: This is a condition where the coat starts to become sparse, progressing to baldness. Dogs are more susceptible to sunburn and there may be secondary skin infections. It affects fawn and blue-colored Chihuahua, though many dogs of these colors have normal coats. Research into the mode of inheritance is on-going.

Pattern Alopecia: Patches of thinning hair and baldness appear in a symmetrical fashion around the temples of the face, the underside of the neck, on the chest and abdomen, and the back of the thighs, usually at around six months. The skin may darken and become scaly.

Corneal dystrophy

This is a late onset condition which can occur in Chihuahuas at any age from 6 to13 years. It affects the cornea, the clear outer layer of the eye, with a build up of fluid, sometimes resulting in painful corneal ulcers. The eyes may appear blue or cloudy and there will be a progressive loss of vision.

Glaucoma

This is an inherited condition where the eye is subject to intraocular pressure which damages the retina and optic nerve, leading to blindness. The Chihuahua is more likely to be affected by secondary glaucoma, which occurs when there is an abnormal layer of tissue within the drainage angle of the eye.

Early detection is essential, as medication and/or surgery can be effective.

Hydrocephalus

This is an abnormal build up of fluid within the cavities of the brain. There is a breed disposition towards this condition because of the shape of the Chihuahua's head. Severely affected puppies die shortly after birth. Others show signs, such as reduced learning ability, failure to develop and seizures before they are three months. If the condition is mild, it can be controlled with medication.

Legge perthes disease

This is a condition where the ball of the thigh bones dies before the skeleton matures, resulting in pain and lameness. It is generally seen in puppies aged four to six months. Early diagnosis, rest and pain relief may help, but surgery is often recommended.

Patellar luxation

This is a condition where the kneecap (patella) slips out of place or dislocates. The kneecap moves in a groove at the lower end of the femur (thigh bone). Some dogs – mostly small breeds – are born with a groove that is not deep enough to retain the kneecap so that it pops out of place.

The characteristic sign is when a Chihuahua hops for a few paces, and then resumes his normal gait when the kneecap slips back into position. It is usually spotted in puppies when they are between five and ten months of age. Sometimes both legs are affected, and if the dog is also overweight, the effect can be crippling.

Surgery may be needed in severe cases but generally a Chihuahua will live with this condition and be largely unaffected, although arthritis may occur in the stifle in later life.

Mitral valve disease

This is a heart condition where blood leaking through the mitral valve can be heard as a murmur when a dog is examined with a stethoscope. Signs include intolerance to exercise, coughing and breathlessness and, at worst, heart failure may result. Treatment will depend on the severity of the case.

Tracheal collapse

This is caused by a malformation of the windpipe, causing the airway to collapse, thereby restricting airflow into the lungs. It primarily affects Toy breeds, and the average onset is around six years of age.

It is often characterised by a honking cough, and is more evident when a Chihuahua is excited, or when he is pulling against his collar. In some cases, a Chi may cough when he tries to eat or drink.

Treatment is needed to suppress the cough and inflammation. Using a harness rather than a collar is also recommended.

Summing up

It may give the pet owner cause for concern to find about health problems that may affect their dog. But it is important to bear in mind that acquiring some basic knowledge is an asset, as it will allow you to spot signs of trouble at an early stage. Early diagnosis is very often the means to the most effective treatment.

Fortunately, the Chihuahua is a generally healthy and disease-free dog with his only visits to the vet being annual check-ups. In most cases, owners can look forward to enjoying many happy years with this affectionate and highly entertaining companion.

Useful addresses

Breed & Kennel Clubs
Please contact your Kennel Club to obtain contact information about breed clubs in your area.

UK
The Kennel Club (UK)
1 Clarges Street London, W1J 8AB
Telephone: 0870 606 6750
Fax: 0207 518 1058
Web: www.thekennelclub.org.uk

USA
American Kennel Club (AKC)
5580 Centerview Drive, Raleigh, NC 27606.
Telephone: 919 233 9767
Fax: 919 233 3627
Email: info@akc.org
Web: www.akc.org

United Kennel Club (UKC)
100 E Kilgore Rd, Kalamazoo,
MI 49002-5584, USA.
Tel: 269 343 9020
Fax: 269 343 7037
Web:www.ukcdogs.com/

Australia
Australian National Kennel Council (ANKC)
The Australian National Kennel Council is the administrative body for pure breed canine affairs in Australia. It does not, however, deal directly with dog exhibitors, breeders or judges. For information pertaining to breeders, clubs or shows, please contact the relevant State or Territory Body.

International
Fédération Cynologique Internationalé (FCI)
Place Albert 1er, 13, B-6530 Thuin, Belgium.
Tel: +32 71 59.12.38
Fax: +32 71 59.22.29
Web: www.fci.be/

Training and behavior
UK
Association of Pet Dog Trainers
Telephone: 01285 810811
Web: http://www.apdt.co.uk

Canine Behaviour
Association of Pet Behaviour Counsellors
Telephone: 01386 751151
Web: http://www.apbc.org.uk/

USA
Association of Pet Dog Trainers
Tel: 1 800 738 3647
Web: www.apdt.com/

American College of Veterinary Behaviorists
Web: http://dacvb.org/

American Veterinary Society of Animal Behavior
Web: www.avsabonline.org/

Australia
APDT Australia Inc
Web: www.apdt.com.au

For details of regional behaviorists, contact the relevant State or Territory Controlling Body.

Activities
UK
Agility Club
http://www.agilityclub.co.uk/

British Flyball Association
Telephone: 01628 829623
Web: http://www.flyball.org.uk/

USA
North American Dog Agility Council
Web: www.nadac.com/

North American Flyball Association, Inc.
Tel/Fax: 800 318 6312
Web: www.flyball.org/

Australia
Agility Dog Association of Australia
Tel: 0423 138 914
Web: www.adaa.com.au/

NADAC Australia
Web: www.nadacaustralia.com/

Australian Flyball Association
Tel: 0407 337 939
Web: www.flyball.org.au/

International
World Canine Freestyle Organisation
Tel: (718) 332-8336
Web: www.worldcaninefreestyle.org

Health
UK
British Small Animal Veterinary Association
Tel: 01452 726700
Web: http://www.bsava.com/

Royal College of Veterinary Surgeons
Tel: 0207 222 2001
Web: www.rcvs.org.uk

www.dogbooksonline.co.uk/healthcare/

Alternative Veterinary Medicine Centre
Tel: 01367 710324
Web: www.alternativevet.org/

USA
American Veterinary Medical Association
Tel: 800 248 2862
Web: www.avma.org

American College of Veterinary Surgeons
Tel: 301 916 0200
Toll Free: 877 217 2287
Web: www.acvs.org/

Canine Eye Registration Foundation
The Veterinary Medical DataBases
1717 Philo Rd, PO Box 3007,
Urbana, IL 61803-3007
Tel: 217-693-4800
Fax: 217-693-4801
Web: http://www.vmdb.org/cerf.html

Orthopaedic Foundation of Animals
2300 E Nifong Boulevard
Columbia, Missouri, 65201-3806
Tel: 573 442-0418
Fax: 573 875-5073
Web: http://www.offa.org/

American Holistic Veterinary Medical
Association
Tel: 410 569 0795
Web: www.ahvma.org/

Australia
Australian Small Animal Veterinary
Association
Tel: 02 9431 5090
Web: www.asava.com.au

Australian Veterinary Association
Tel: 02 9431 5000
Web: www.ava.com.au

Australian College Veterinary Scientists
Tel: 07 3423 2016
Web: http://acvsc.org.au

Australian Holistic Vets
Web: www.ahv.com.au/